Your All-In-One CV and Job Search Companion

Conquer Internet Overwhelm and Land Your Dream Job

LAURA HARMSWORTH

Contents

Foreword

If you're looking for a new job, having a well-written CV is essential. A great CV will highlight your skills and experience, and hopefully land you an interview.

Sadly, too many jobseekers lose opportunities thanks to their CV. They don't know the tricks and strategies you need to write a professional, modern CV and don't have an expert to write one for them.

That expert is CV writer extraordinaire Laura Harmsworth. I have known Laura for over five years through my website, talentedladiesclub.com. Laura has written several helpful articles about CVs for us and has even launched the British Association of CV Writers.

I can't think of anyone more qualified to write this book. Laura has years of high-level experience in CV writing, and is passionate about raising standards in the industry and helping more people open doors with the right CV.

I can't recommend highly enough following Laura's advice in this book and wish you luck on your job-hunting journey.

Hannah Martin

Founder, Talented Ladies Club

talentedladiesclub.com

Introduction

If you're writing or updating your CV, consider these questions.

- Have you tried talking about yourself, your abilities?
- Do you enjoy writing about and selling yourself, or do you
- feel like you're bragging?
- Have you become frustrated? You have amazing experience
- and want to show it all off, but can't fit it all onto your CV.
- Is your CV four pages long? To get your CV to two pages have you extended the margins to their max or minimised the font to an unreadable 8?
- Does your CV contain information that you are rightly proud of but is not relevant to what you want to do next? Do you know what to cut out and how?
- Are you tired of spending endless hours scrolling through countless (often conflicting or out of date) online resources in search of the perfect CV advice?

Look no further! Welcome to "Your All-In-One CV and Job Search Companion" - the culmination of my years of experience as a CV writer and founder of the British Association of CV Writers.

My early career was in HR, working for the NHS then a telecoms company, providing support in recruitment, training, and all things HR. After a career break, I returned to work part-time, focusing on graduate recruitment for investment banks and law firms. It was during this time that I realised the need for better support in crafting CVs and helping individuals sell themselves effectively. Caversham CV Writing was born in 2012.

Since then, I've supported hundreds of individuals in creating or improving CVs that have led to interviews and job offers. I also share my expertise through articles for a local newspaper.

In this book I've condensed all this knowledge and experience into one comprehensive resource to spare you the endless scrolling and searching online. It will equip you with the essential tools and strategies needed to create a compelling CV and cover letter, optimise your LinkedIn profile, and prepare for interviews.

Say goodbye to endless scrolling and start your journey towards job search success today.

Connect with me

LinkedIn: www.linkedin.com/in/lauraharmsworth
Facebook: www.facebook.com/CavershamCVWriting

Note

The advice in this book refers to CVs for the UK market. Please check specific requirements for other countries.

Templates and tools

You have access to several templates and tools in this book that are stored on a Google Drive.

Look out for these symbols:

Tools   **Templates**

You can access them at:

www.cavershamcvwriting.co.uk/tools-and- templates/

Password: cvbook

To save or download your own editable copy

When the documents are saved on your device, any changes you make will only be visible to you. Don't worry, I won't be able to see any of your edits.

If you use Google Docs

- Sign in to your Google account and open the document
- Go to 'File' and then 'Make A Copy' to create your own
- version of the file
- Save it to your Drive

If you don't use Google Docs

- Open the document
- Go to 'File' then 'Download'
- Choose your file format and it will download to your computer

Chapter 1: What type of CV should I use?

Did you know there's more than one type of CV format? All showcase your skills, experience, and achievements, but in different ways. Here I provide a summary of four types of CV and why you might choose them.

Reverse chronological

This is the CV you're probably most used to seeing or using.

Everything is written in reverse chronological order with your most recent experience and qualifications showing first.

This CV is logical and makes it easy for recruiters to see your experience and progression.

This format is for you if you've been following a natural career path.

Functional (also known as skills-based)

This format focuses the reader's mind on what you can offer in terms of skills, abilities, and professional expertise, rather than in which role you acquired them.

By putting your achievements and contributions under a "Skills and Achievements" heading you can highlight your transferable skills and so employment gaps and irrelevant experience are less obvious.

Under the "Career History" section, list each job with little to no detail underneath.

For example, you have managed projects in several of your roles. Put all your project management experience and achievements under the heading of "Project Management" in the "Skills and Achievements" section, rather than under each role.

This format is for you if you're changing career direction or have a career gap. Just be aware that recruiters are often wary of this type of CV.

Hybrid

A functional CV isn't favoured by all recruiters and hiring managers so a hybrid of functional and chronological works well.

The "Skills" section can be more informative, to include examples and achievements but not to the extent of a functional CV. You will keep a lot of that information under reach role.

An advantage of a hybrid CV is that all key information is on page 1.

This format is for most job seekers and particularly suits those just starting out, changing careers, or returning after a career break.

One page

One page CVs are quick and easy to read but it can be tricky deciding what to include and they lack the detail required when applying to an advertised role.

They do have their place though e.g. your employer might ask you when tendering; you're self-employed and need to show what you can offer in terms of experience and skills; you have limited work experience.

If you're a student, see Chapter 11 for a template you can use.

 Templates

Reverse chronological CV
Functional CV
Hybrid CV

Chapter 2: What sections should my CV include?

There aren't set rules in CV writing but there are guidelines. Here is an outline of what to include on, and exclude from, your CV.

Personal Details

- Name
- Headline (your current or targeted role)
- Town and county (full address not needed)
- Contact number/s
- Email address
- LinkedIn URL

You don't need:

- A title of "CV" as its obvious what the document is
- Date of birth
- Marital status
- Religion
- Photo
- Driving licence (unless requested on job ad)

Profile

- Short, interesting, and tailored to the role applying to
- Four to five lines
- Relevant experience, knowledge, qualifications, training, and personal attributes
- Personality (you can write this section in the first person)

Key skills

- Four to six relevant skills: ensures the recruiter can easily see them
- Depending on the CV format you choose, this might be a bulleted list with just the skill or a more detailed bullet with a line or two demonstrating how you evidence the skill

Career history

- Don't include everything about every role you've had - every single thing you include on your CV must be relevant to the role you're applying to
- If you have a lot of experience, and the last 10 years are relevant, flesh these out and reduce the information on anything older (unless relevant)
- For those with a lot of experience or worried age might go against them, add an "Early Career" section with job titles and companies, leaving out the detail and the years worked there (see chapter 12)

Voluntary roles

- Include if the role adds value to your CV by showing transferable skills or it fills an employment gap

Education, training, and qualifications

- Relevant training: dates, name of course/qualification, and institution
- Students and graduates should add this section before the Career History/Work Experience section

Interests

- It's personal preference if you want to include interests - I suggest only adding activities that are relevant to the role or industry, are particularly interesting, show your personality or values, or are a good talking point at interview

Footer
- Page number and name in case CV is printed and pages get separated
- Don't include important information here such as contact details

References

- No need to include as it will be assumed you have these

Chapter 3: What are my skills and how do I use them in my CV?

Recruiters see hundreds of CVs and when you apply they're looking to see if your skill set matches the role requirements.

Your CV must therefore have the relevant key skills for that role littered throughout it. If you're changing career, focus on your transferable skills (see Chapter 9).

How to identify your skills

- Seek input from others e.g. family, friends, colleagues, coach/mentor
- Find adverts for your ideal role e.g. Indeed or LinkedIn
- Highlight the skills, write them into a document, group them, and delete duplicates/ones you don't have
- Take a personality questionnaire. The results can highlight key personality attributes, help you focus on suitable career paths, recognise motivations and blockers, and highlight strengths and weaknesses. I recommend www.16personalities.com (the free services are perfectly adequate)

Use the skills worksheet to collate your skills.

What to do with your skills list

List the top four to six skills in the "Key Skills" section of the CV to ensure they stand out to the recruiter and are picked up by ATS.

If you are using a bulleted list of simply the skills without elaboration, you can show them in columns:

- Write the skills as a bulleted list
- Highlight your list
- Go to Layout, Columns, and pick two or three depending on the number of skills you've chosen and how long they are

Litter the skills throughout your CV i.e., in the profile and career history sections. Don't do this for the sake of it, make sure it reads well and every skill is backed up with an example or achievement.

 Tip

Keep your skills worksheet updated as your career progresses.

 **Tool**

Skills worksheet

Chapter 4: I don't like selling myself so how do I do this on my CV?

Achievements are a key part of your CV, proving you have the skills and abilities the recruiter is looking for and that you can deliver results. Can you solve their problems, impact the bottom line, increase efficiency, decrease costs, or improve customer service?

Many CVs read like job descriptions, with responsibilities and no achievements, often because people cannot think of achievements or they don't want to appear arrogant.

Don't worry that by adding your achievements you're overselling yourself - by quantifying them they are proven i.e., not just your opinion.

For example, instead of writing "Responsible for company website" rephrase to "Increased enquiries by 15% by rewriting company landing page."

Here are the steps you can take to do this.

Gather your achievements

Think through all your roles and write down:

- Positive feedback
- Awards
- Targets achieved

- Things you have implemented or actioned that have
    - saved money
    - reduced resources
    - improved profit, customers, sales, enquiries
- Challenges overcome

Brainstorm

Write as much as you want on each achievement using the STAR (Situation, Task, Action, Result) or CAR (Context, Action, Result) technique. This is a good interview preparation exercise too!

Here's an example:

Situation: As a senior customer service manager, our latest feedback poll showed customer satisfaction had dropped significantly.

Task: At our monthly senior management meeting I was asked to investigate the causes of the drop and what could be done to bring the levels up.

Action: I collected all the data and customer comments on why they were dissatisfied and reviewed with my customer service team leaders, asking for their input. I devised ways of improving on these areas e.g. more regular product training of customer service staff; reviewing customer feedback more regularly to ensure issues are resolved more quickly.

Result: Within a month, customer service had increased by 20%.

Refine

- Turn each achievement into a succinct sentence or two
- Lead with the result (the R in STAR and CAR) to grab attention, then follow with actions taken
- Start with a positive action verb e.g. increased, implemented, developed, improved, won (see chapter 7)
- Quantify where possible e.g. percentages, number in your team, how often you perform a task

For the customer service manager example, the refined achievement would be:

Increased customer satisfaction by 20% in a month by analysing customer feedback, seeking input from the team, and implementing new measures such as more regular training.

If your achievements aren't quantifiable, consider when you have:

- developed a client relationship
- renewed contracts
- worked on specific projects (objective, results)
- streamlined a procedure
- negotiated a discount
- presented to an audience
- avoided fines
- kept up to date records
- met audit requirements

Put all your achievements in a document (see tool below), copy and paste the ones relevant to the job ad into your CV, and use further examples and detail from the document at interview.

 Tip

Keep a "base" CV with all your achievements on, then tailor a copy of it for each role, selecting the most relevant achievements for that role.

**Tool**

Achievement tracker (with a video to explain how to use it).

Chapter 5: Meet the robots

ATS is Applicant Tracking Software and is used by recruiters to:

- Manage and track candidates
- Parse information from a CV into data fields
- Identify strong matches

It will typically scan:

- Key words from the job ad and job description
- Job titles
- Degree
- Structure

Don't be afraid of ATS or listen to the scaremongering. It has improved over the last few years so some of the old recommendations no longer stand. However the following are good guidelines to follow when writing your CV, whether a recruiter uses ATS or not.

Skills and key words

- Pull together job advert, job description, emails from recruiters
- Highlight hard skills e.g. project management, data analysis
- Highlight soft skills e.g. collaboration, customer service
- Highlight action verbs e.g. lead
- Use the words and skills that you can evidence in your CV

Ensure you can back each of these up with an achievement or example and that they make sense where you place them i.e. don't just add them for the sake of it.

Job title

Match this as closely as possible to the role being advertised and change if it is honest to do so and makes sense e.g. Executive Assistant – Personal Assistant.

Use standard job titles e.g. if your current role is Brand Warrior and you're applying to be a Marketing Manager, use the latter.

Include this title as a headline under your name at the top of your CV.

Qualifications and certifications

Only include those that are relevant and if a job ad uses an acronym, include that too.

If a job ad asks for a specific qualification that you don't have, apply directly rather than online if possible.

Formatting

- Standard serif or sans serif font e.g. Arial, Tahoma, Georgia, Lucinda, Calibri, Verdana, or Trebuchet
- Font 10-12 throughout (name can be larger)
- Black text on a white background (plus one optional colour e.g. for title headings)
- Standard circle bullets and standard headings
- No tables, columns, graphics, logos. Have a separate CV with these for direct or offline applications
- Long-form as well as acronyms
- Consistent date formats: 09/2023 or September 2023 (include month)
- One-inch margins

- No headers or footers
- Save your CV as .doc, .docx, .rtf, or .pdf – check if the job ad or recruiter asks for a specific file type

 Tip

Jobscan (www.jobscan.co) provides ATS simulation using your CV and a job advert. The website also has a wealth of resources about ATS and CV writing.

 Tip

Correct spelling and grammar enable ATS to pick up the right skills and keywords, and recruiters get a good first impression of you. More on spelling and grammar in the next chapter.

Chapter 6: Spelling and grammar

"My spelling is Wobbly. It's good spelling but it Wobbles, and the letters get in the wrong places."
-- A. A. Milne

Whilst you might forgive Winnie the Pooh for the odd typo, a recruiter will be less forgiving if they find one on your CV.

Checking spelling and grammar sounds so simple and obvious but it's often what lets a CV down, despite impressive content. According to a survey by Adzuna in 2019, a review of 20,000 CVs submitted online found that 9 in 10 of them had misspelled words.

Rightly or wrongly, if a recruiter has a pile of good CVs on their desk, this can be one way to eliminate a handful.

What should you do?

- Run spellcheck but don't rely on it. It won't pick up errors such as manger for manager and might Americanise words so keep an eye out for those e.g. organization, specialized
- Double-check all grammar, particularly apostrophes e.g. GCSEs and KPIs don't need apostrophes
- Use the Read Aloud function in Word. Hearing the text will enable you to pick up typos that spellcheck doesn't
- Print off your CV and read it
- Ask someone else to read it
- Read it backwards (sounds odd but it works!)
- Have a night's sleep (or at least an hour or two break from looking at it), then read it again
- Use tools such as Grammarly (a free app you can use to check documents) and Hemingway Editor

Chapter 7: Every word matters - are you being positive?

Positive action words are dynamic and make your CV come alive. You want your CV to make an immediate impact – the average reader will form an impression within 6-20 seconds and might not carry on reading after that. Every word matters!

Using positive action verbs on your CV rather than passive words express action and infer that you'll make an impact in the role and to the company.

- Don't start every line with "Responsible for" – remember it's about your achievements not your responsibilities
- Use the strongest action/power word you can find at the beginning of a sentence to ensure your CV is impressive
- Avoid jargon words
- Don't overuse the same phrases or words (see tip below)
- Ensure the action verb is relevant to the key words in the job advert/description

There's a good list of action verbs here (just beware of the Americanisation):

www.thesaurus.com/e/writing/resume-action-verbs/

 Tip

Use the synonym function of an online thesaurus e.g. if you type in "influenced", options include determined, shaped, and persuaded.

Chapter 8: Can I use the same CV for each application?

My answer to this question is a resounding "No"!

As stated in the previous chapter, recruiters typically spend 6-20 seconds scanning a CV so yours needs to showcase how you fit the advertised role.

Your CV must be tailored to every role you apply for. Writing a generic CV and using it for numerous applications without changing the content is unlikely to land you an interview.

The hiring manager wants to know how you fit the bill specifically and what you can bring to the company.

If you submit a generic CV, the reader will have to assume certain things, read between the lines, or think you're a poor match. Spend time tailoring every application - believe me, it will be worth it!

How to tailor your CV

- Read the job advert– the skills and knowledge section on the job ad in particular (if there is one) will help you identify what they are looking for
- Highlight all the parts of it you have experience of and add to your CV, in your own words but using as much of their terminology as possible
- Ensure the skills and key words identified are littered throughout your CV
- Only include relevant responsibilities or those that demonstrate transferable skills they're looking for.
- Put the most relevant experience at the top of each role. If

you led a small team for one of your roles a few years ago but this is not a requirement for the job applying for, leave it out. If you apply for another role where team leadership is an essential or desirable skill, keep it in

- For each skill you need to provide proof you have it, and achievements are the ideal way to do this. It's crucial to prove what you can do by quantifying your abilities through your achievements (see chapter 4). Include the relevant achievements under each role that match what is being looked for.

 Tip

Your CV is your advert, not your life story. This can be hard as there is a lot of emotion tied up in your work history and this makes it hard to decide what to put in, what to minimise, and what to leave out. You might be rightly proud of an achievement, but if it's not relevant to the role you are applying for, leave it out.

 Tip

I suggest keeping a "base" CV on your computer, and tailoring it for each role so you always return to the original CV. For each section, you can have an unlimited list of bullet points that build up over the time of your job search and career. When you tailor your CV choose which ones are suitable for a role and tailor them specifically to that role using those good old key words and putting the most relevant things at the top of each role.

Chapter 9: Career changes

In a 2019 study by Jobrapido, nearly two thirds of the UK workforce wanted to change their career path and when Totaljobs conducted a survey of 5,364 British people affected by coronavirus, it found one in five used their free time in lockdown to search and plan for a career in a new industry.

Switching industry can be really daunting - your job is to show a recruiter what makes you a good candidate for the role compared to someone who is already in the industry.

Which career?

Spend time considering your options and the impact on your lifestyle, family, finances, mental health, happiness etc.

Do you want to work more from home or are you happy to commute?

What makes you tick, what are you passionate about?

Consider working with a career coach to help you define your next move.

Research

Research is key to confirm whether an industry and role are for you, and to demonstrate your commitment to a career change.

- Speak with contacts
- Shadow someone in the industry
- Read relevant news articles
- Subscribe to journals and podcasts

- Attend events
- Secure a voluntary role
- Connect with relevant people and companies on LinkedIn
- Investigate required qualifications (e.g. for teaching, healthcare, IT, engineering, and law)
- If a less formal qualification is required, find training for little cost that will fit around other commitments e.g. Udemy, Skillshare, LinkedIn learning (LinkedIn often do a free trial)

Update your CV and LinkedIn profile

Update your CV with the key transferable skills required that you have from paid and voluntary roles, and ensure the experience and achievements are tailored to the new industry.

A hybrid or functional CV would be the best layout to use.

Chapters 3, 4, and 8 will help you with writing your CV for a career change,

Update LinkedIn (see chapter 15), stating you're changing industries and ensure your skills and experience on your profile are matched to what the industry requires. You can do this in the "About" section (adding Key Specialities), put the keywords in your career sections and update the skills list (you can have 50 skills).

Chapter 10: Mind the Gap! What do I do if I have a career gap?

You may be surprised by how many people have gaps in their career, be that due to raising a family, being made redundant, illness, or a life choice such as travelling.

Don't be worried about any gaps, just ensure you explain them in a positive manner.

If you have resigned or been made redundant and not gone straight into another role, rather than highlighting this, add things to your CV that you have done such as:

- Voluntary work
- Training
- Assisting a friend to set up a business
- Hiring a career coach
- Reading trade journals

As well as boosting your knowledge, skills, and confidence, these will show you in a positive light and demonstrate that you used the time well.

If you don't have anything to add, start doing something now. Upskilling is a great thing to do - even if you can demonstrate that you have enrolled on a course that hasn't yet started, this is something to add to your CV and will help fill a gap.

Tip

There are some great websites that provide free or low cost online courses including coursera.org, futurelearn.com, udemy.com, open.edu, skillshare.com, alison.com, and online-learning.harvard.edu. If you want a certificate or accreditation, you will need to check if these are provided.

Another option is LinkedIn Learning. You can access this if you sign up for a free trial of LinkedIn Premium (remember to cancel at the end of the trial period if you don't wish to continue with the paid plan). As well as gaining access to the courses, you're also able to direct message recruiters, see who has viewed your profile, and gain job applicant and salary insights. With LinkedIn Learning, you can add training badges to your profile.

Remember, there's nothing wrong with a gap on your CV as long as you explain it.

Chapter 11: Student CVs

Much of what I have covered is suitable for a student CV but there are some differences students should be aware of. Below is an overview of what sections to include and their order.

Remember, employers are looking for potential at this stage of your life as much as experience.

Personal details

You can include a home address and a term-time address.

Profile

In the absence of any or little experience, emphasise your energy and ambition, and non work-related skills and experience that demonstrate your suitability e.g. babysitting, gardening for neighbours, team projects at school, or being part of a sports team.

Education

Include subjects, level, institution, and dates.

Add in projects, awards, and modules (particularly if relevant to the type of role applying to).

Your grades might not be what you were expecting but don't worry. You don't have to add in specific grades and can put that you achieved passes in or studied English, Maths etc.

Work experience and voluntary roles

You'll have less experience than those who left school a few years ago so you need to make the most of what you've done. Think about your interests too and how these can showcase a skill e.g. blogging.

Focus on what you learnt and what you contributed. Were you:
- Praised
- Placed in positions of trust
- Given extra responsibilities

Have you:
- Solved any problems
- Contributed to a team
- Worked on your own initiative

Example: Increased circulation of the school magazine by 10% on the previous year, by introducing the use of social media.

Continuously seek to improve this section through voluntary work, work experience, holding a role in a club/society, or being on the school council.

Awards and certifications

Include Duke of Edinburgh, music and dance grades, sports achievements, first aid, lifeguarding, and refereeing, for example, all show commitment, interest, and build your skills.

 **Template**

Student CV

Chapter 12: Job search tips for the over 50s

Ageism is still a thing in today's job market, so how can you overcome some of the barriers to your job search?

The tips below will help draw attention to what you offer and your value, rather than your age.

CV

- Use a simple fresh format and a modern font e.g. Calibri
- Don't include your date of birth
- Summarise your key relevant experience, transferable skills, and technical abilities if relevant in the "Profile" section
- Use an "Early Career" section, without dates, for anything more than ten years ago. Only include the last ten years in detail (unless something is particularly relevant in your earlier roles)
- Exclude anything you're skilled in that is outdated technologically
- Consider a functional or hybrid CV instead of the typical reverse chronological CV so the focus of page one is on your skills and achievements
- Create or update your LinkedIn profile and add this to your CV – keep the profile up to date and engage on the platform, demonstrating you're up to date in communicating and networking (see Chapter 15)
- Use a current email e.g. Gmail

Training and development

- Ensure you're up to date with skills relevant to your role and also more generic tools such as video conferencing
- Demonstrate your desire and ability to learn new skills by attending courses and adding these to your CV and LinkedIn profile

Cover letter

- Demonstrate your up-to-date knowledge in a cover letter - show you understand the most pressing issues in your field. Read books, articles, and the news, and listen to podcasts. This shows you're engaged and will help during networking/at interview
- State that you are willing, eager, and able to learn new skills and give examples of where you have done this
- Be succinct (one page is fine) and don't use older style language or styling e.g. one space after a full stop rather than two

Interview

- Plan what you will wear – look at current employees of the company on LinkedIn/company website and see if there's a general trend
- If interviewers suggest you're overqualified, you can respond that you don't see yourself as overqualified but that you have a wealth of expertise to bring to the company and can add value. Highlight a couple of the responsibilities on the job ad and explain what excites you about them and how you will bring value

- Be forward looking – recruiters don't want to see that you have achieved everything you've wanted to – plan an answer for "where do you want to be in five years' time?"
- If you haven't had an interview for a while, have a couple of run throughs with a friend or family and use the STAR (Situation, Task, Action, Result) technique. Prepare a bank of examples and achievements that are relevant to the role you are interviewing for
- Use body language and your smile to show your energy and positivity

Networking

You will likely have contacts from a wide variety of backgrounds, get in touch with them stating the type of role you're looking for. If your network is small, attend groups and events, get on LinkedIn, and start engaging.

Chapter 13: You've written your CV – what next?

Stay informed

Keeping up to date with the job market and company information is important when job hunting. Here are some suggestions on how to do this.

LinkedIn

- Follow relevant people and companies – keep an eye on employee movement, mergers, creation of new departments as these could all lead to new vacancies
- Connect with people in the industries and companies you're interested in (sending a personalised note with the connection request is a positive thing to do)
- Check your feed daily

Facebook and Instagram

Not just for teenagers, updating your friends and families with your activities, or following celebrities, these sites can be extremely useful if you're looking for a job.

Companies are using these platforms to highlight their achievements, new products, and their culture - all of value when determining if you'd like to work for a company, for inclusion in your cover letter, and for discussion at interview.

- Search and follow the companies you'd like to work for
- Look at how they post, what they post, and how they respond to comments
- If you have something relevant and of substance to add, get involved in the discussion (but don't engage just for the sake of it)
- By following thought leaders in the industry you can learn all sorts of things and see what the latest trends and hot topics are

X (formerly Twitter)

This is a great way to learn as well as engage and show your personality to potential recruiters and hiring managers.

- Follow relevant industry twitter handles for job openings and news
- Search hashtags e.g. #Hiring #NowHiring #Jobs #Careers #JobOpening #JobListing #JobPosting and industry-specific ones e.g. #TechJobs
- Create regular and meaningful content, not just retweets
- Link to your LinkedIn profile, blog, etc.
- Don't be overly formal – show your personality

Look for jobs

Aside from registering with job boards, agencies, and applying to adverts, there are other ways to find a job.

You may have heard of the hidden job market and wondered what it is. It's not a mystical place like Diagon Alley but refers to job opportunities that aren't advertised and filled through other means.

These job openings are not publicly posted for various reasons, such as maintaining confidentiality, not tipping off current employees, or saving time and resources.

So what can you do to find jobs that are advertised and not advertised?

Your current employer

If you enjoy working for your current company, discreetly find out if there are different roles becoming vacant in the near future.

Networking

- Make a list of everyone you know from all areas of your life and work your way through them (colleagues, family, friends, alumni, associations, professional associations) – you never know who they know
- Say you're seeking advice as you're looking for a job (be specific with the type of role) – are you asking them for a reference, asking for industry insights, do they know of anything in this area
- Don't be worried about asking – it's human nature to like being asked for advice/to want to help someone; most people nowadays have been in the situation of looking for a role so will understand
- Reciprocate – this is all about building and maintaining mutually beneficial relationships for now and in the future. Thank your contact for any advice received, ask about them, can you send them any relevant information for their role,

perhaps an article you've read recently, can you introduce them to someone else in your network?

- Keep in touch - keeping in touch with your network throughout your career (not just when job searching) is positive for so many reasons including sharing ideas and industry and company insights
- Check LinkedIn daily
- See chapter 15 for more on networking on LinkedIn

Classifieds

I remember as a student, trawling through the classifieds section of newspapers looking for a job, circling the ones that took my fancy then giving them a call or printing off my CV to hand deliver or post.

Traditional print ads still exist and can be a good place to look, as can trade journals and magazines. As an aside, if you work or would like to work in a specific industry, I'd recommend signing up to the relevant industry journals. They will keep you abreast of current news and trends – this will help you decide if you'd like a role in the industry and will also prove useful at interview.

Online job boards

Online job boards are another useful tool – you can use them to search for relevant skills when writing your CV, see what is available in the area you're interested in, and upload your CV to the ones you like the look of.

Here are some examples:

- Guardian Jobs
- Indeed (largest global jobsite)
- Monster (another large global jobsite)
- Totaljobs (another large jobsite)

- CVW Jobs (IT)
- WorkInStartups and AngelList (startup jobs)
- Ladders (managers)
- Flexjobs (remote roles)
- Scouted (college graduates)
- Snagajob (hourly workers)
- Adzuna (aggregates roles from various sources)
- Glassdoor (to check out employers)

As with anything online, there are risks and Get Safe Online has some tips here:

www.getsafeonline.org/personal/articles/job-searching/

Careers fairs

Have you attended a careers or job fair?

I have, as a CV writer, a few years ago. Here are some of my tips:

- Find out which companies are going and target the ones you're interested in
- Tailor your CV to your targeted company and role (you might need more than one version)
- Compile a list of questions you'd like to ask
- Prepare and practise a short intro about yourself
- Take printed copies of your CV (high-quality paper) and/or personal business cards
- A notebook and pen will be handy so you can jot down any thoughts from each company (or use voice notes on your phone)
- Dress smartly

- Ensure there's room in your bag for any brochures you pick up (and pens and sweets!)

Contact companies directly

Research their website, values, current news, see if you have any warm contacts who currently or used to work there (LinkedIn is invaluable for this).

Then get in touch, ready to outline your relevant skills and achievements that are beneficial to them.

Find out if they are looking for volunteers if you're in a position to do this. This will give you experience, a chance to see if the company is a good match, and to be among the first to hear of vacancies.

Keep up with the news

Listen to and watch national channels and check your feed daily on LinkedIn. Do you see a company struggling with an issue you could contribute to solving? If one of their pain points falls within your expertise, get in touch.

Google Alerts is a handy tool. Type in the company and key employees you want to hear about and you'll get notified when Google has new content. You can use this to learn about possible vacancies through new office openings, mergers etc. and you can use the updates to talk about when you call the company about vacancies, and then at interview.

Prepare a cover letter that can be tailored to each application

Whether asked for or not, I always recommend you send a letter to accompany your CV.

This should be one page and it's a great way to convey your passion for the role and company you're applying to.

You can also explain gaps, career changes, and other situations to set the scene for the information laid out on your CV. The next chapter covers this in more depth.

Interview preparation

This is all about the preparation – company research (info, values, news items, strategy, and direction), reading the job ad and description to identify key skills and achievements that back up your suitability, what to wear, how to get there, and background and tech for online interviews.

See chapter 16 for more guidance.

**Tool**

Job board list

Chapter 14: Cover letters

I'm often asked if a cover letter or email is required when sending your CV to a recruiter or hiring manager. I suggest writing a cover letter whether it's asked for or not. Your letter or email should:

- Introduce you to an organisation, explain your motivation for applying, and highlight your key relevant skills
- Illustrate your level of written communication skills - check your spelling and grammar and don't use text speak
- Be tailored to each application

Top tips on how to write a cover letter

- Keep to one page
- Include your name and contact details
- State the role you're applying for. If you're applying speculatively, tell the company what area of the business you'd like to work in and why
- Talk about what attracts you to the role and the company – read the news, business reports, website, values, social media
- Highlight the three key skills they're looking for and write a sentence or two about how you match this with your experience, voluntary work, training, and interests
- Thank them for reading your letter, state your CV is attached, and that you look forward to hearing from them
- Close with 'Yours sincerely' if you have used their name, otherwise use 'Yours faithfully'

 Template

Cover letter

Chapter 15: Are you a LinkedIn lurker?

If you are and you're job seeking, you need to stop being a lurker and become an engager!

A high percentage (I've seen 70% quoted in several places) of jobs are secured through networking, rather than an advertised role. LinkedIn is a fantastic place to network and is often under-utilised by jobseekers. There are over 30 million employers on LinkedIn and over 20 million open job opportunities.

A key point is that your LinkedIn profile is different from your CV. Your CV is tailored to a specific role but your LinkedIn profile speaks to many potential employers. You can add so much more to your LinkedIn profile, including a bit more personality, colour, emojis, presentations, other media, and links to articles you've published.

LinkedIn enables you to add up to 50 skills to your profile, get these skills endorsed, and ask for recommendations.

LinkedIn brings your career history to life!

Here are my tips for the key sections of your profile.

Photo

Your profile picture is your first impression on LinkedIn, so it's crucial to make it count. Profiles with a picture receive 21 times more profile views than those without.

You can create a great profile pic at pfpmaker.com and LinkedIn gives you the options to add a filter and adjust the brightness and contrast.

Guidelines for your photo:

- Just you
- Looks like you now (not 15 years ago)
- Head and shoulders filling 60% of the photo
- Neutral background
- Well-lit from the front with no shadows on the face
- Smile and look approachable
- Recommended size is 400x400 pixels

Banner

The banner image at the top of your profile is prime real estate to showcase your personality and skills. Stand out by creating a customised banner using a tool like Canva: www.canva.com/linkedin-banners/templates

A unique banner can make your profile more memorable – don't settle for the default one.

Profile URL

LinkedIn often provides you with a default URL containing random letters and numbers.

Clean it up as follows:

- Click on the "Me" icon
- Select "View Profile"

- Click "Edit public profile & URL"
- Edit the last part of your URL to include your name
- Click "Save"

Remember to add the updated URL to your CV.

Headline

This is the line under your name and defaults to your current job title. Stand out by using all 220 characters (at the time of writing) to highlight what you do, your expertise, and your interests.

If you're using the mobile app, you can add an extra 20 characters.

About

This is your opportunity to tell your professional story and inject some personality.

- Avoid long paragraphs; instead, use emojis, and bullet points, and vary your sentence structure
- Steer clear of starting every sentence with "I"
- Share key achievements and specialities
- Include a call to action.

The character limit at the time of writing is 2600.

Experience

This section should effectively communicate your professional journey and achievements.

- Use bullet points instead of large blocks of text to make it reader-friendly and engaging
- Include keywords relevant to your industry and the specific job you're seeking

Skills list

You can add up to 50 skills to your profile and according to LinkedIn, users with five or more skills are contacted up to 33 times more by recruiters.

Ensure you list skills that are relevant to the industry and job that you're targeting. To optimise your skills section, review several job advertisements in your field and industry to identify recurring keywords. These keywords should also be strategically placed throughout your profile.

Get these skills endorsed by colleagues and ask for recommendations.

All-star status

This will mean your profile will be found by more people and recruiters. A bar at the top of your profile will highlight actions you can take to attain this.

Once your profile is up to date, what should you do?

Once you've optimised your LinkedIn profile, it's crucial to keep it up to date, even when you're not actively job searching. Networking and staying visible on the platform can lead to unexpected career opportunities.

- Follow relevant people and companies: keep an eye on industry leaders, influencers, and companies of interest. This helps you stay informed about trends and opportunities – great for finding roles and for interviews
- Check your feed daily; engage with and write posts: share insights, articles, or thoughts related to your field. Engaging with others' posts and writing your own can enhance your visibility and credibility
- Ask for endorsements and recommendations: politely request endorsements for your skills from connections who can vouch for your abilities. In return, offer to endorse their skills as well. A recommendation is a commendation written by another LinkedIn member and can be requested from your first degree connections you work with or have worked with
- Update your profile with relevant keywords: whenever you come across a job posting that aligns with your interests, highlight key phrases and incorporate them into your profile
- Experiment with your headline: change your headline every three to four weeks and monitor how it impacts your visibility in search results
- Include your LinkedIn URL in email signatures: add your LinkedIn profile link to the footer of your email communications, making it easy for recruiters and hiring managers to connect with you
- Regularly review and update: keep your profile error-free, professional, and aligned with your current career pursuits

Tip

LinkedIn has a detailed presentation on how to make the most of LinkedIn that I highly recommend reading. It is the one entitled "LinkedIn for jobseekers" and there's some other great info on the site:

https://socialimpact.linkedin.com/lifg-resources/linkedin-training-content

 Tip

LinkedIn also offers a premium career subscription, which comes with several features that can assist your job search:

- Direct message recruiters: reach out directly to recruiters and hiring managers
- See who's viewed your profile: identify potential connections and opportunities by viewing who has checked out your profile
- View applicant and salary insights: gain insights into job applicants, including their education, current roles, and more
- Access courses via LinkedIn Learning: improve your skills and knowledge by taking advantage of LinkedIn Learning courses

You can try LinkedIn premium career for free with a 30-day trial. Just remember to cancel if you decide not to continue, as it costs around £30 per month (at the time of writing).

Chapter 16: My top interview tips

Here are my top tips on how to prepare for an interview.

Days and weeks prior to the interview

- Read the advert, job description and person specification thoroughly
- Think of situations and projects where you can demonstrate what is being asked for. Have ready an example from your experience for each key skill/competency
- Research the company: ensure you have a good awareness of the company you are applying to – competitors, market, customer base, recent news, structure, values, key personnel. Look at their website and annual report. Try to speak with someone in the company to gain useful insights and a feel for the company
- Make notes about your current / most recent role and company: business type, business goals, how you worked to the business goals, culture, how this compares to new company, what you could bring from this company to new role
- What are your future plans: think of your career goals, where this role could lead you, and what you need to do to reach next goal
- Prepare a potted history: think about your education and career to date, overview of choices made and how jobs led from one to the next; be prepared to explain any gaps in your CV

- Plan your outfit: base this on your personality and the type of organisation you're interviewing for; ensure all clothes are clean, ironed, and your hair is neat
- Think of questions you might be asked (the first five points will help with this)
- Prepare a list of questions you'd like to ask at the interview

Example questions to ask

- How will I be appraised and my performance reviewed?
- What scope for progress and promotion is there for me within the company?
- Can you describe your ideal employee?
- Could you explain the company structure to me?
- How many other people will I be working with in the team?
- What are their job roles?
- Are there any skills gaps within the team that I could address?
- What do you like about working at the company?
- What makes this company stand apart from the competition?
- What are the company's plans for the future?
- Do your employees socialise outside of the workplace?
- Can you describe what a typical day or week for me in the job would look like? Does the job role have any pressing concerns that need to be addressed by me immediately?
- What challenges might I face in this position?
- Does the job involve any form of training?
- Will I be expected to work late nights or at the weekend?
- Will the job involve much travelling?
- When are you looking for someone to start?
- Would you like any additional information from me?
- Do you have any questions about my ability to do this job?

- When can I expect to hear from you?

The night before

- Prepare a document holder with copies of your CV, job description, documentation if asked for, pen and paper to take notes
- Check where you need to go and where there's parking if you're driving
- Try to get a good night's sleep

Interview day

- Allow plenty of time to get to the interview
- Turn off your mobile phone
- Make eye contact with the interviewer and have a firm handshake
- Answer the questions and don't waffle
- If you don't know the answer, don't make it up, it is alright to say you haven't come across that before, but you'd be interested in learning more about it
- Don't be negative about current or former employers
- Leave the interview in the same polite, assured manner in which you entered – look the interviewer in the eye, smile, and give a firm handshake

Online interviews

<u>Prepare yourself</u>

- Find out as much as you can on what to expect e.g. who will be on the video call (unless it is a pre-recorded interview), what platform the interview is on e.g. Zoom, Teams, Skype, Facetime, Google Hangouts

- Check you can use the technology on your laptop (preferable to a phone). It's worth setting up a practice meeting with a friend or family member to test your camera and speaker, and to make sure that you can share your screen in case you are asked to do a practical task
- Conduct research on the company and industry by looking at their website and social media. Create a list of questions to ask and prepare answers to questions you think could be asked. Ensure you have your achievements/examples at the ready
- Prepare in advance what to wear

Prepare the room

- Do this a couple of days before the interview, not five minutes
- Choose a location that is quiet, with no distractions
- Clear any clutter and ensure pictures / books on shelves are suitable
- Face a window instead of a wall, turn off overhead lighting, and put a lamp on a table behind you
- Check your location has a strong and stable internet connection
- Turn off your mobile phone and close down applications on your laptop

Practise

- Search online e.g. Glassdoor for some common interview questions and practise – either with a friend or family member, or by recording yourself and watching it back
- When watching yourself back, look out for any mannerisms you can change e.g. constant fidgeting, looking at the screen rather than the camera, talking too fast

- You can split your screen, so you have the video call on one side and any prompts on the other. Don't read directly from your notes

 Tip

Always send a thank you note to the interviewer/s after a face to face or online interview. Ensure it is genuine, enthusiastic, and tailored to that interview.

Chapter 17: Following up on a job application

We've all been there and it is one of the most frustrating and demoralising parts of job seeking. You've invested lots of time and effort into submitting an amazing CV and cover letter, then regularly hit the refresh button on your inbox or eagerly await the postie for details of the anticipated job interview.

Often it feels as though your application has disappeared into an abyss, never to be heard of again.

- Did my CV get lost?
- Did I leave out my contact details?
- Am I no good at what I do and no one wants to employ me?

These are the thoughts that may run through your head.

Why have you not heard?

The recruitment process usually consists of a few stages. Your CV might be run through Applicant Tracking Software, then sent to one or more recruiters or hiring managers, before finally being passed back down the chain asking someone to invite you to the next stage. The reasons are many and sometimes you'll never find out.

Actions to take

To make you stand out from the crowd and to gain a higher chance of getting feedback (if you don't get an interview, it's good to know why for your next application), it's a great idea to follow up on the application.

It demonstrates your enthusiasm and interest in the role as well as putting your mind at rest regarding some of the worries mentioned above. It could also set you apart from other candidates who have similar experience and qualifications to you.

In a survey of over 300 UK employers, conducted by Reed, 82% of recruiters indicated that it reflects well on a candidate when they get back in touch.
However, don't overdo it both in terms of timing and how you execute the follow-up. Two weeks is a good time to wait and don't get back in touch more than a couple of times.

Email

This is a good method as you both have a record of what you have sent and recruiters can respond at a time that suits them.

- Send your email from a professional email address (consider setting up an email account purely for your job search)
- Keep it short and professional
- Put the title of the job you have applied to in the subject line, then write a few sentences to thank them for taking time to read your application and ask if they have questions regarding your experience
- If you have accomplished anything within your role or gained a new qualification since your original application, you can include this here, but not too much information; the email should be quite short
- If you have any questions regarding the application process, ask this before signing off
- As with your CV and cover letter, spell check and proofread the email before firing it off

Phone

This is more of a direct approach and some could find it intrusive, but in other industries e.g. sales, hiring managers could see this method as a positive.

- Be polite, friendly, and enthusiastic
- Introduce yourself and ask if they have received your application and when they will be making their decision
- If they haven't yet decided, you have a better chance of sticking in their mind. You can also ask if they need any clarification on your application or any further information. If they have decided and it is a "No", now is the time to ask for feedback
- End the call on a positive note and thank them for their time
- It's a good idea to practise what you are going to say before making the call, ensuring you are clear and don't speak too quickly
- If you phone and are greeted with the answering machine, leave a clear, succinct message including your name, contact details and title of the job you have applied for

LinkedIn

Firstly, ensure your LinkedIn profile is bang up to date.

- If you have the name of the recruiter, consider adding them to your LinkedIn network or messaging them through LinkedIn. This also allows you to demonstrate your network and endorsements
- Your message will be similar to the email content above – subject line, reaffirming your interest in the role and company, asking if they require clarification or more information, and thanking them for their consideration.

Letter

Do people write letters anymore? Certainly not to the degree they used to, and this could work in your favour as it adds a personal touch, shows your interest, and could help you stand out from other applicants who follow up using other methods.

- The letter can be handwritten or typed, consist of a few succinct sentences and as above, thank them for their time and consideration
- If appropriate you could include a professional business card with the letter
- Send the letter first-class post as it shows you place importance on sending the letter
- As with your CV and cover letter, spend time on the presentation and format. You can create a document similar to personalised stationery e.g. name/address as a header; phone/email details as a footer. Ensure the letter is well spaced and use a font such as Arial or Calibri – matched to what you have used for your CV
- Include the date, contact name, and address of where you are applying for and put the title of the role you are applying to as a subject line

How you decide to follow up depends on your preference, the culture of the company you are applying to, and the industry.

What is key is that you shouldn't wait for them to get in touch - what do you have to lose?

Remember, if you don't get this job, your perfect job is out there, it just requires a bit of patience but will be worth it in the end!

⚒ Tool

Keep on top of the progress of your applications with the job search tracker.

Chapter 18: Keeping positive

Here are my top tips for maintaining positivity whilst applying for jobs.

Choose your space and time

- Find a dedicated space if you can with plenty of natural light
- Make this space pleasant to work at e.g. add a plant or a photo and light a candle
- Ensure your table and chair are as ergonomic as possible
- Don't work whilst on the sofa with the TV on, or in bed
- Work at a time that suits you best and stick to a routine as much as possible. I'm a morning person, so as soon as the children have left for school and college, and the house is tidy, I'm at my desk

The 10-minute rule

I'm a real fan of this - if I have a task I've been putting off, I use this rule.

Tell yourself you'll just spend ten minutes on this task and you'll more than likely find that you either get it done in that time, have made a great start so feel more positive about it, or get to the end of the ten minutes and carry on as you've got into the right mindset.

Take regular breaks

This is important for two reasons – your productivity and mental health. Go for a walk, hang out the washing, post a letter.

My preference is to have a break outside to get some sunlight and fresh air (I appreciate this is harder when the weather isn't so great but don your wellies and a coat and you'll be surprised how much better you feel when you get home).

There are apps you can use to remind you to take breaks e.g. www.geckoandfly.com/34644/take-a-break-reminders/

Stay in touch

Maintain contact with others, professional and personal.

You know yourself best and how much time you need on your own or with others – ensure you're getting the contact you need, be that on the phone, via Zoom or in person. Don't feel guilty about stepping away from online applications to walk to the local café to meet a friend.

As well as the health benefits, by maintaining your network, you never know where this will lead in terms of a job.

Switch off

Choose a time you will stop working on your applications and stick to it.

Turn off your computer and put it out of sight if possible. Don't be tempted to log back on to check for any updates, wait until tomorrow.

You might not want to use all these suggestions, what works for one person doesn't work for another, but hopefully at least one of these tips will make your time applying for a job a bit easier and more pleasant.

Chapter 19: Positive actions you can take after a redundancy

For the final two years of my career in HR, I spent the majority of my time supporting the business and employees through redundancies. I then went on maternity leave and instead of returning to work, I took voluntary redundancy.

For me, this was a positive experience as I was in control and made the decision; it was what I wanted. It enabled me to stay home and bring up our children, and to start Caversham CV Writing.

For many though, redundancies can be negative and are out of their control.

My experience in redundancies, both during my time in HR and now by supporting people with key job search tools, means I've seen a range of emotions and reactions so can empathise if you're on that rollercoaster at the moment. Try to remember it isn't personal.

Of the people I speak with, some are receiving outplacement support from their company, others aren't. Some feel dejected, others see this as an opportunity to reflect on their career and a time to make a change. There are those for whom this has been on the horizon for a while, and for others it is a bolt out of the blue.

Whatever your situation, there are actions you can take.

Check out your rights

Check your company's redundancy policy and the ACAS website to ensure you're receiving the correct entitlements and support.

There's also good advice about your finances here: www.moneyadviceservice.org.uk/en/articles/out-of-work-checklist-things-to-do-if-you-lose-your-job

Decide on your future direction

Remember redundancy isn't your fault and it's the role that's being made redundant.

Take some time out if you can, to recover and reflect. Don't start applying for lots of jobs the day you're made redundant. Have a good think about what you want to do and what you're good at.

- Take a personality questionnaire (there are some good, free ones available) or engage the services of a career coach
- Make a list of your skills (including the transferable ones), key experience, and key achievements (see chapters 3 and 4)
- If your finances allow, you can undertake some training or volunteer to increase your skills base/address any skill gaps, whilst applying for jobs. There's plenty of free training available e.g. FutureLearn, Udemy, Skillshare, and you can often sign up to a month's free trial with LinkedIn Learning

Update your CV

The majority of people don't keep their CV updated as they're focusing on doing their job. Suddenly, you now need your CV!

Working through this book will help you, particularly the section on career gaps which shows you the things you can do and add to your CV including training, voluntary, reading relevant journals, listening to podcasts, attending online events, and hiring a career coach. All these will show you in a positive light and demonstrate that you used that time well.

If you don't have anything to add to this section, start doing them now. Upskilling is a great thing to do - even if you can demonstrate that you have enrolled on a course that hasn't yet started, this is something to add to your CV and will help eliminate a gap.

Sign up to job boards

Sign up to as many online job boards as you can and register with relevant recruitment agencies.

Utilise your network

Job boards are great but tapping into your network is invaluable. If you're not on LinkedIn, create a profile and if you're on there, ensure your profile is up to date and start networking (see chapter 15).

Keep positive

This is important when writing your CV and at interview. Don't talk about the redundancy or your former employer negatively. Show you're in a position to move on and aren't resentful.

Remember, there are many things in life we have no control over and redundancy is one of those. What you can control is how you react to it and the actions you take.

I hope these practical ideas help you through this period of your life and make you feel more in control.

Chapter 20: Should I use a CV writer?

Many people write their own CV with successful results whilst others need support. How can a CV writer help you and what should you look out for?

External perspective

You're not alone if you find it hard to define and talk about your abilities and achievements, or to decide what to include and take out from your CV. A CV writer will pull out the key points to highlight in your CV and help recruiters see why they must employ you – without making you sound arrogant.

Getting past the robots

You can have the best experience, the most amazing achievements and be the perfect person for the job – but your CV might not reach the next stage if it's not written in the right way and doesn't include key words. Good CV writers understand how ATS works but won't scaremonger you about it as a reason to get them to work with you.

Time

It's easy to think that you're saving money by writing your CV yourself but crafting the perfect CV takes time. CV writers don't need to research how to write a CV and will save you time so you can focus on what you do best. The time you do spend with them going through your experience, skills, and achievements will be time well spent as it will help with interview preparation and often builds confidence.

My tips for finding a CV writer that suits you

- Call to discuss your requirements – does the writer instill confidence?
- Are the prices in your budget? Ensure there are no hidden extras
- Check their website, social media, testimonials, presence on LinkedIn, do they have plenty of experience?
- Speak with a few so you're sure you are working with someone who understands you and what you want to do next
- Are they a member of the British Association of CV Writers? Members have passed a CV test and agreed to a Code of Ethics and continuing professional development

Chapter 21: Is AI the future of CV writing?

Artificial Intelligence (AI) is a term we're hearing more of but if you've not heard of it, here's a brief outline from a luddite!

There are a few chatbots including OpenAI's ChatGPT and Google Bard. These understand and generate answers to text questions, like a friendly robot. They have been trained on large amounts of data including from the internet, books, and social media. I'll refer to it as ChatGPT as it's the only one I've played around with (I got some good menu ideas!) and is the most common.

One way it's being used is in generating CVs and cover letters. You can give ChatGPT the job description/advert that you want to apply to, and your CV, and ask it to optimise your CV around the key words.

Benefits

- Generates text, ideas, and guidance
- Takes seconds to create content
- Assists in overcoming writer's block and can improve writing by suggesting different words and phrases, similar to a thesaurus.
- Identifies key words from the job description and advert
- Checks for typos and grammar (use alongside spell check, Read Aloud, Grammarly, and other methods outlined in chapter 6).
- Free/low cost

Limitations

- Unemotional and lacks creative skills so won't capture your voice, personality, and context
- Can fabricate points about your experience and qualifications
- A human CV writer will delve deeper and ask the right questions
- Data privacy concerns
- Plagiarism – if you copy and paste content for your CV from ChatGPT without making any changes, it won't sound like you and recruiters may well detect this and/or use one of multiple tools that detect the use of chatbots

My thoughts

Whilst AI has a place in writing your CV, use it with caution and as a tool to assist you. You can start with AI suggestions to help guide you, add your personal touch, then run through AI again to check for typos. I would suggest that AI is not yet at the point where it can fully replace a human in writing a CV. I'd love to know your thoughts!

Chapter 22: Career coaches

Many people come to me seeking help with their CV but they don't know what role they want next.

I always refer them to a career coach first, as having a targeted CV will improve their chances of success. I'm a firm believer in accessing the support of coaches - they can work with you to identify the right role for you and help with the transition, amongst many other things.

There are many career coaches out there and it's important you take the time to find one that is a good fit. It is an investment in terms of time and money so you need to ensure you'll have a good relationship and your requirements will be met.

Here are some pointers when looking for a career coach:

- Ask for recommendations and check out LinkedIn recommendations and Trust Pilot reviews
- Check the Career Development Institute's register of career professionals
- See if the career coach is accredited and therefore up to date with best practice
- Arrange a call with a few – you'll be sharing some possibly confidential information with your coach so want to ensure a good fit, that you will trust them, and your communication styles are matched

If you prefer to go down the DIY route, there are a multitude of books you can buy. I recommend:

- What colour is your parachute? (Richard Bolles)
- The squiggly career (Helen Tupper and Sarah Ellis)
- Career Coach: How to plan your career and land your perfect job (Corinne Mills)

Conclusion

By following the advice in this book and using the tools and templates, you should have a strong interview-generating CV and cover letter (remember to tailor them to every single application), an up to date and optimised LinkedIn profile, and are feeling confident about interviews.

If you want to ensure you've actioned everything, use the job search checklist which is over the page or download it via the Tools and Templates link.

I'd love to hear how you get on!

Laura
contact@cavershamcvwriting.co.uk

Job search checklist

Preparation

☐   Coaching sessions or books if required

☐   Skills worksheet completed

☐   Achievement tracker completed

CV: Heading

☐   Excluded "CV" or "Curriculum Vitae", DOB, or photo

☐   Name in bold and larger font

☐   Headline

☐   Town and County

☐   Contact number/s

☐   Email

☐   Customised LinkedIn profile URL

CV: Profile

☐   Section heading "Profile"

☐   Four to five lines

☐   Succinct, sells you, not wishy washy

☐   Tailored to role applying to / ideal role

☐   Personality shines through

CV: Key Skills

- ☐ Four to six key skills drawn from the job advert / description
- ☐ Bulleted list in columns or more detailed bullet points

CV: Career History

- ☐ Job title, company name and location, dates (mmyyy–mmyyy)
- ☐ A line about the company
- ☐ One to two lines outlining role and key responsibilities
- ☐ Key Achievements – STAR or CAR, starting with the Result
- ☐ Action verbs included
- ☐ Reverse chronological order
- ☐ Included and explained any gaps
- ☐ Previous roles, written in past tense.
- ☐ Current role, written in present tense.
- ☐ Tailored to role applying to / ideal role

CV: Voluntary Experience

- ☐ Include if adds value/explains a gap in paid employment

Education / Education and Training / Education and Qualifications

- ☐ Qualification title, institution, date achieved
- ☐ Only include things from years ago if asked for in job advert
- ☐ Reverse chronological order

CV: Interests

☐   Include if particularly interesting or relevant to the role

CV: References

☐   No need to include as it will be assumed you have them ready

CV: Personal

☐   Do not include DOB, marital status, religion

☐   Include driving licence if asked for in job

CV: General

☐   Black text, plus one optional colour

☐   Sans serif / web safe font, size 11-12

☐   Circle bullets

☐   No tables, graphics, photos, logos

☐   Limited use of bold, italics, underlining

☐   Clear and simple layout, with plenty of white space

☐   Two pages, unless reducing to two takes out key information

☐   Consistent use of headings

☐   Consistent date format

☐   Consistent use of font

☐   Full stop at end of every sentence

☐   Write in long-form any acronyms the first time used

CV: Spelling and Grammar

- ☐ Spellcheck
- ☐ Word's Read Aloud
- ☐ CV printed and read (and read again after a break)
- ☐ Someone else has read CV
- ☐ CV read backwards
- ☐ Grammarly / Hemingway Editor

Cover Letter

- ☐ Tailored to role
- ☐ Details changed e.g., date, job title applying to

LinkedIn

- ☐ Photo
- ☐ Banner
- ☐ Profile URL customised and added to CV
- ☐ Headline
- ☐ About
- ☐ Skills list of 50
- ☐ All-star status

Interview

- ☐ Company research
- ☐ Achievements prepared (relevant to role)
- ☐ Potted history and future plans prepared
- ☐ Questions to answer
- ☐ Questions to ask
- ☐ Interview practice
- ☐ Outfit prepared
- ☐ Travel prepared
- ☐ Documents in a folder with pen and notebook
- ☐ Technology prepared (online interview)
- ☐ Room prepared (online interview)
- ☐ Thank you note sent
- ☐ Job search tracker updated

About the author

Laura Harmsworth

With a background in HR and training for the NHS, a global telecoms company, investment banks, and law firms, I've seen a lot of CVs!

After a career break I focused on CV writing and founded Caversham CV Writing in 2012.

My achievements to date include:

- Master's degree in human resource management
- CV writer since 2012
- Founder and Chair of the British Association of CV Writers
- Mentor at Queen Mary, University of London

I live in Reading, Berkshire, with my husband, our three teenagers and Molly the Cavapoo – there's never a dull moment in our house!

Printed in Great Britain
by Amazon